Simply Christmas

Easy Dramas, Speeches, and Recitations for Children

Compiled and edited
by
Peg Augustine

 Abingdon Press

CONTENTS

LET'S GET READY

Production Notes

You may choose to perform this play with a children's chorus singing "An Angel Told Mary" and "Holy Baby, Holy Child," while other children walk on and off for the scenes; or, you may have the entire cast on stage and let them do the singing, simply stepping forward to say their lines. You may use as many or as few angels, shepherds, and wise men as you have children. Simply combine speaking parts to use fewer characters or divide speaking parts for more characters.

The costumes and set can be as simple or as elaborate as you choose. Children enjoy dressing up as biblical characters, but if you cannot manage costumes, make headdresses for each character (wraps for Mary, Joseph, the innkeeper, and the shepherds; sparkly tinsel halos for Gabriel and the other angels; crowns for the wise men); angels could hold stars fastened to dowels; shepherds may hold staffs or crooks; and wise men might carry small treasure chests or beautiful bottles.

Characters

Narrator
Mary
Joseph
Innkeeper
Gabriel
Shepherds
Angels
Wise Men

Scene One

Chorus or cast sings "An Angel Told Mary."

NARRATOR: It was just like any other day. Mary was busy with her work, probably thinking about the day she would marry Joseph. Then suddenly, as quick as you can blink, an angel appeared. Mary did not know what to think.

5

GABRIEL:	Greetings, favored one. The Lord is with you. Do not be afraid. You are going to have a baby and you will name him Jesus. Your baby, Jesus, will be called the Son of God.

Scene Two

Chorus or cast sings "An Angel Told Mary." Mary and Joseph walk onto stage.

MARY:	Joseph! Is it really you? I was afraid you would never want to see me again.
JOSEPH:	Mary, I have been so upset these past few days. I thought and thought and then decided that I would end our engagement quietly and not talk to you again. But I have something important to tell you.
MARY:	Oh, Joseph, since you are here, I have something important to tell you, too; but I am not sure you will believe me. I can hardly believe it myself.
JOSEPH:	I will believe you, Mary.
MARY:	You will? But you haven't heard my story yet.
JOSEPH:	Mary, whatever your story is, it's fine with me. Listen. While I was asleep last night—I hardly even know how to tell this—Mary, I was visited by an angel.
MARY:	Joseph! That's what I was going to tell you. I was visited by an angel, too! Only I wasn't asleep.
JOSEPH:	Mary, tell me exactly what happened to you. I want to hear all about it.

MARY: Well, it was an ordinary day. I was doing housework when suddenly he was in the room with me. I didn't see him come in, so I was a bit shocked. Then he said, "Greetings, favored one! The Lord is with you."

JOSEPH: Favored one! Then it's got to be true!

MARY: What does?

JOSEPH: I'll tell you in a minute, but go on.

MARY: I thought it was a strange greeting, but he told me not to be afraid. He said, "You have found favor with God. You will bear a son, and you will name him Jesus." I asked how I could possibly be going to have a baby since I am not married. The angel said that all this would happen because of the power of the Most High and that the baby will be called the Son of God. Joseph! The baby must be the promised Messiah!

JOSEPH: Yes! Yes! That's exactly what the angel told me in my dream. He said, "Joseph, son of David, do not be afraid to take Mary as your wife. The baby she will have is from the Holy Spirit. You must name the baby Jesus, for he will save his people from their sins!" Oh, Mary, this is exciting!

MARY: But, Joseph, I'm scared. How can I be a mother to the Messiah? How will I know what to do?

JOSEPH: Don't worry, Mary. I will be right by your side. And God will help us know how to be good parents. That angel brought us both good news.

Chorus or cast sings "Holy Baby, Holy Child."

Scene Three

NARRATOR: Several months later a Roman messenger came to Bethlehem. "Hear this, hear this!" he said. "Every man must be counted. You must go to the home of your ancestors to be registered." When Joseph heard the messenger, he hurried to tell Mary about the new law.

MARY: Joseph, you are one of the descendants of King David. That means we will have to go to Bethlehem, the city of David. That's a very long way.

JOSEPH: I know. I wish we didn't have to go, but it is the law. I am worried. It will be a hard trip for you. It is almost time for our baby to be born.

MARY: Don't worry. God will take care of us.

NARRATOR: The trip from Nazareth to Galilee was long and dirty. The roads were crowded with people going to to be registered. When night came they had to sleep on the ground under the stars. Finally they arrived in Bethlehem. Mary and Joseph could hardly believe what they saw. The streets of Bethlehem were even more crowded than the road they had traveled on had been. Joseph did not want Mary to have to sleep outside another night. Surely the baby would come soon. Mary needed shelter!

JOSEPH: Here is an inn, Mary. It looks pretty crowded, but I'll see if they have a space for us.

INNKEEPER: I am sorry. There is no room in my inn. But there is one place. It's a stable, just a small cave really. You'll have to share it with the animals. But there is soft hay there and it will be warm. Your wife won't have to sleep outside.

JOSEPH: Thank you, thank you.

NARRATOR: Joseph and Mary made their way to the cave where the animals stayed. After long nights of sleeping along the road, the stable looked like a king's palace. And indeed, it was a king's palace. For that night in the stable, the long-awaited Savior, God's Son, was born. Mary wrapped the baby in bands of cloth while Joseph made a bed in the hay in the feeding trough.

MARY: Thank you, God, for taking care of us.

JOSEPH: Thank you, God. We will take good care of your Son.

Chorus or cast sings "Away in a Manger."

Scene Four

NARRATOR: It was a cold night on the hillside near Bethlehem. The sheep had been counted and were safely in their folds. The shepherds gathered near the campfire to keep warm. It was a dark night; and the shepherds lay quietly listening to the *baa*s of the lambs and the crackling of the campfire.

Suddenly bright light and beautiful music was everywhere! One by one the shepherds sat up, startled from their dreams by the unexpected brightness of the star that lit up the sky.

SHEPHERD 1: What's that?

SHEPHERD 2: What's happening?

ANGEL: Do not be afraid. We have come to tell you good news of great joy for all the people. Tonight a baby was born in Bethlehem. He is the Messiah, the Savior of the world.

SHEPHERDS: (*ad lib*—What? Huh? Where? *and so on*)

9

NARRATOR: The shepherds were amazed. They wondered what they should do, and then the answer came.

ANGEL: You will find the baby in Bethlehem. He is wrapped in bands of cloth and lying in a manger.

ANGELS: Glory to God and peace to all the earth.

SHEPHERD 1: Did you hear that? What does it mean?

SHEPHERD 2: Let's go to Bethlehem. Let's go see the Savior.

NARRATOR: The shepherds hurried away to Bethlehem where they found the newborn Jesus.

SHEPHERD 1: Praise God! We must tell everyone about this wonderful thing. We must tell everyone that the Savior has come!

Congregation sings "While Shepherds Watched Their Flocks."

Scene Five

NARRATOR: Even before Jesus was born in Bethlehem, some wise men from the East had been watching the sky to learn about the world. Then one night a very bright star appeared in the heavens.

WISE MAN 1: Stars? I have seen a lot of beautiful stars. In fact, I have spent my life studying the stars. But there was one star that was more beautiful than all the rest. I was looking at the sky one night—like I always do—and there it was. I had never seen such a star before. It was big and bright. I knew that this star was a sign that something special had happened.

WISE MAN 2: I talked to others who studied the skies. They had seen the star, too. We were sure that it was a sign that the King of the Jews, the one who would be the Messiah, had been born. We had to follow the star. If the star was telling us that the Messiah had been born, we knew that we had to go to worship him.

WISE MAN 3: First we went to Jerusalem. Surely the King of the Jews could be found in Jerusalem. King Herod called for the Jewish priests and scribes. They told us that according to the Scriptures the King of the Jews would not be born in Jerusalem, but in Bethlehem. King Herod told us to go and find the child so that he could come and worship him, too. So we traveled on. And that special star led us. It stopped right over the house where the young child Jesus was.

WISE MAN 4: We were overwhelmed with joy! We fell to our knees and worshiped the child we knew was the Messiah. And then we opened the gifts we had brought him. The gifts were the best we had—gold, frankincense, and myrrh.

WISE MAN 5: When we were ready to go back home, we remembered that King Herod wanted to know where to find Jesus so that he could come and worship, too. But in a dream God warned us not to tell Herod. Herod did not really want to worship Jesus at all. Herod was jealous because he wanted to be the only king. So we decided not to tell Herod where Jesus was. We left Bethlehem and went home by another way.

WISE MAN 1: A beautiful star? Yes, I saw the most beautiful star of all.

Congregation sings "Joy to the World."

GO, SHEPHERDS! GO, SHEPHERDS!

Production Notes

Children may clap and snap their fingers in rhythm to this story-poem. It will probably take several practice sessions for them to become proficient. Print the words on posterboard and let the children read the words. You may even want to let the children read during the actual performance. Encourage the children to speak clearly and crisply. Another alternative would be for an adult or a group of teens to read the poem while the children clap and snap.

Ho, shepherds! Ho, shepherds!
Clap, snap, snap, clap, snap, snap,
Guarding your sheep,
Clap, clap, clap, clap,
Watching the starry night
Clap, snap, snap, clap, snap, snap,
While others sleep.
Clap, clap, clap, clap.

Count, shepherds! Count shepherds!
Clap, snap, snap, clap, snap, snap,
Those in the fold.
Clap, clap, clap, clap,
Do lambs sleep warmly a-
Clap, snap, snap, clap, snap, snap,
gainst the night's cold?
Clap, clap, clap, clap.

Look, shepherds! Look, shepherds!
Clap, snap, snap, clap, snap, snap,
Shading your eyes.
Clap, clap, clap, clap,
What is that brilliance that
Clap, snap, snap, clap, snap, snap,
Brightens the skies?
Clap, clap, clap, clap.

Hear, shepherds! Hear, shepherds!
Clap, snap, snap, clap, snap, snap,
What is that voice?
Clap, clap, clap, clap,
Bringing good news, saying
Clap, snap, snap, clap, snap, snap,
"Shepherds, rejoice!"
Clap, clap, clap, clap.

Heed, shepherds! Heed, shepherds!
Clap, snap, snap, clap, snap, snap,
Hear the voice say,
Clap, clap, clap, clap,
"Born is a savior to
Clap, snap, snap, clap, snap, snap,
You on this day."
Clap, clap, clap, clap.

"Look for this sign, shepherds!
Clap, snap, snap, clap, snap, snap,
Do not fear danger.
Clap, clap, clap, clap,
You'll find Messiah, a-
Clap, snap, snap, clap, snap, snap,
sleep in a manger."
Clap, clap, clap, clap.

Bow, shepherds! Bow, shepherds!
Clap, snap, snap, clap, snap, snap,
Hosts all around
Clap, clap, clap, clap,
Praise God in heaven, and
Clap, snap, snap, clap, snap, snap,
Echo the sound.
Clap, clap, clap, clap.

Go, shepherds! Go, shepherds!
Clap, snap, snap, clap, snap, snap,
Ere time has flown.
Clap, clap, clap, clap,
Search for this thing which the
Clap, snap, snap, clap, snap, snap,
Lord had made known.
Clap, clap, clap, clap.

There, shepherds! There, shepherds!
Clap, snap, snap, clap, snap, snap,
You've found the way.
Clap, clap, clap, clap,
Worship the baby a-
Clap, snap, snap, clap, snap, snap,
sleep on the hay.
Clap, clap, clap, clap.

Now, shepherds! Now, shepherds!
Clap, snap, snap, clap, snap, snap,
Praise and be bold.
Clap, clap, clap, clap,
Tell all who'll listen what
Clap, snap, snap, clap, snap, snap,
You have been told.
Clap, clap, clap, clap.

by Sharilyn S. Adair

REJOICE!

READER 1: "Greetings, the Lord is with you," the angel said to Mary. "For nothing will be impossible with God."

ALL: *(Sing "An Angel Told Mary.")*

READER 2: "Here am I," said Mary, "the servant of the Lord; let it be with me according to your word."

READER 1: "Blessed are you," said Elizabeth, when Mary told her about the blessing she was to receive. And Mary rejoiced and praised God.

ALL: My soul magnifies the Lord, and my spirit rejoices in God my savior.

READER 2: "We must go to Bethlehem," said Joseph, "for we must pay our taxes."

READER 1: "No! There is no room!" said the innkeeper. "There is only one place for you to stay."

READER 2: So Jesus was born in a stable and had to sleep on the hay.

ALL: *(Sing stanza 1 of "Amen.")*

READER 2: "What is happening?" said the shepherds in the fields nearby. For they were frightened by the glory of the Lord that shone from the sky.

READER 1: "Do not be afraid," said the angel. "I bring you good news of great joy."

READER 2: And the angel told the shepherds about the new baby boy.

READER 1:   "Glory to God," said the heavenly host. And the angels and shepherds rejoiced.

ALL: *(Sing "Glory!")*

READER 1:   "Let us find the newborn child," said the shepherds. And they went to find the baby lying in a manger.

READER 2:   "Praise God, praise God," said the shepherds as they left the stable where Jesus was born. "Praise God for all we have seen and heard."

READER 1:   "See the star," the wise men said. "It tells of the birth of a king."

READER 2:   "Let's find the king so that we may worship him," they said. And they started on their journey from the East.

READER 1:   "Accept our gifts; receive our praise," the wise men said when they found the child.

ALL: Opening their treasure chests, they offered him gifts of gold, frankincense, and myrrh.

Reader 1:   Praise God, praise God, we say today. Thank you for sending Jesus. Thank you for the good news of great joy!

ALL: *(Sing "Glory!")*

SHEPHERDS SEE JESUS

Production Notes

This little drama can be performed with very young children. Let the children dress in biblical costumes and sit in a semicircle to play the chorus. Place a tableau of children representing the holy family and the shepherds near the front of your acting area.

NARRATOR: It was a very dark night. A group of shepherds were sitting around a campfire. (*Crumple scraps of paper to make the sound of crackling fire.*) Some of the shepherds were singing softly to the sheep.

CHORUS: (*Hum a few notes of a familiar Christmas carol.*)

NARRATOR: Most of the sheep were sleeping. Every now and then one of the sheep would make a sound.

CHORUS: Baa. Baa. Baa.

NARRATOR: It was very quiet … when suddenly an angel of the Lord appeared. The shepherds were startled!

CHORUS: Oh! Oh! (*sounding frightened*)

NARRATOR: But the angel said, "Do not be afraid. I bring good news. The Savior has been born in Bethlehem. Go and see him."

CHORUS: Yeah! Yeah! Yeah! (*with excitement*)

NARRATOR: The shepherds ran as quickly as they could into the village.

CHORUS: (*Slap hands on thighs to make the sound of running feet.*)

NARRATOR: When they found the stable, they went in quietly. There they found the baby in the manger.

CHORUS: Ahh! Ahh! Ahh! (*admiring the baby*)

NARRATOR: They gave the baby a gift, a lamb.

CHORUS: Baa. Baa. Baa. (*happily*)

NARRATOR: Mary smiled at the shepherds. She was very happy. She thanked the shepherds for coming.

CHORUS: Thank you. Thank you.

NARRATOR: When they were ready to leave, Joseph followed them to the door. He thanked them once again.

CHORUS: God bless you. God bless you.

NARRATOR: The shepherds were so happy that they ran through the streets shouting. They told everyone what they had seen and heard.

CHORUS: The Savior has come! His name is Jesus!

NARRATOR: The people who had been sound asleep called from their windows.

CHORUS: Be quiet! Be quiet!

NARRATOR: The shepherds laughed with joy and returned to the fields running.

CHORUS: (*Slap hands on thighs to make the sound of running feet.*)

CHRISTMAS TRADITIONS

Production Notes

Depending on the ages of your children, either have the child holding the object explain its significance, or let the child step forward as an older person tells of the object's significance. Children may wear their regular clothes, or you may want to make them costumes from posterboard of the objects they represent.

CONGREGATION, CHOIR, OR CAST*: (Sing verse 1 of "I Heard the Bells on Christmas Day.")*

SPEAKER 1: *(Holds up a bell. For a younger child, you might make a bracelet of jingle bells.)* Long before Jesus was born, bells were used to send messages of special events—both happy and sad. When bells ring joyfully at Christmastime, they announce the good news that Jesus has come. Bells remind us of the Christmas promise of goodwill.

ALL: *(Sing "O Christmas Tree.")*

SPEAKER 2: *(Holds up a small Christmas tree. As an alternative, the lights of a large tree might be turned on at this time.)* There are many stories that suggest how decorated trees have become a part of our Christmas traditions. However, the one common part of the story is the use of an evergreen tree. Evergreen trees remind us of God's everlasting love and of eternal life offered through Jesus.

For a slightly longer program, you might add ornaments to a tree and have the children tell what each ornament represents.

Lights: Lights remind us that Jesus said, "I am the light of the world."

Angels: Angels are God's messengers, who told the good news to Mary, Joseph, and the shepherds.

Candy canes: Candy canes are shaped like the shepherd's staff. Upside down, they form the letter "J" that reminds us of Jesus.

Bells: Bells ring out the good news of Jesus' birth.

Animals: Jesus was born in a place where animals were kept.

Musical instruments: Music is a special way to express joy.

Glass balls: A circle is a symbol of God's never-ending love.

Stars: Stars remind us of the star that guided the wise men.

Gifts: Gifts remind us that Jesus is a gift from God, and that the wise men brought gifts of gold, frankincense, and myrrh.

Doves: Doves are a traditional symbol of peace on earth.

ALL: *(Sing "Come, Thou Long-Expected Jesus.")*

SPEAKER 3: *(Holds up a sprig of mistletoe.)* Mistletoe attaches itself to a tree and gets its life from the tree. Mistletoe reminds us that Jesus is the vine and we are the branches. Our lives get their strength and their meaning from our relationship to God through Jesus.

ALL: *(Sing "I Want to Walk as a Child of the Light" or "O Little Town of Bethlehem.")*

SPEAKER 4: *(Holds up a battery-powered candle.)* Candles remind us that Jesus brought the light of God's love into our world. At Christmas the flickering flames look like twinkling stars, especially the star that guided the wise men to Bethlehem.

ALL: *(Sing "Once in Royal David's City.")*

SPEAKER 5: *(Holds up a sprig of holly.)* The leaves of the holly tree stay green all year round. Legend says that the crown of thorns Jesus was forced to wear before his death was made from holly. The sharp points drew blood that stained the white holly berries red. At Christmastime, holly foreshadows Jesus' death.

ALL: *(Sing "We Three Kings.")*

SPEAKER 6: *(Holds up a wrapped gift.)* Giving gifts did not originate with the wise men who visited Jesus. However, at Christmas we are reminded of the honor paid to Jesus when we give and receive Christmas presents. Our presents are symbols of our love for one another. Our presents are a way of honoring the gift God has given us in Jesus Christ.

ALL: *(Sing "Joy to the World.")*

SPEAKER 7: *(Holds up a giant Christmas card.)* Although there are several stories about when the first Christmas cards were sent, it is clear to us why Christmas cards are important. Christmas cards spread goodwill and joy to the world as we remind one another of the good news of great joy that the angels brought to the shepherds.

PRAYER: Gracious God, we feel your presence so close to us during the days when we are getting ready for the birth of your Son. As the new year begins, let us find more and more ways to serve and honor you. Amen.

THE TWELVE DAYS OF CHRISTMAS

Production Notes

This uses up to twelve children and a narrator. Children will hold the symbol for each day as they speak. Use Christmas ornaments, toys, or cut-out pictures for the symbols. It is possible to purchase ornaments with the symbols on them. If you do this, it would be nice to decorate a small tree.

NARRATOR: You probably think of Christmas as just one day, but in the church "Christmas" refers to a twelve-day period that starts with Christmas Day. This is where the song "The Twelve Days of Christmas" comes from. The world celebrates Christmas for twelve hours, but the church celebrates it for twelve days because the gift of Christ is with us for twelve months of the year.

ALL: (*Sing*) "On the first day of Christmas my true love gave to me a partridge in a pear tree ..."

SPEAKER 1: The "true love" represents God, and the "me" who receives the presents is the Christian. The partridge in a pear tree is a symbol for Jesus Christ who died on a tree as a gift from God.

ALL: (*Sing*) "On the second day of Christmas my true love gave to me two turtle doves ... "

SPEAKER 2: The doves represent the Old and New Testaments, another gift from God.

ALL: (*Sing*) "On the third day of Christmas, my true love gave to me three French hens ... "

SPEAKER 3: The "three French hens" are faith, hope, and love, the three gifts of the Spirit that Paul writes about in 1 Corinthians 13:13.

ALL: (*Sing*) "On the fourth day of Christmas my true love gave to me four calling birds ..."

SPEAKER 4: The "four calling birds" represent the four Gospels which sing the song of salvation through Jesus Christ.

ALL: (*Sing*) "On the fifth day of Christmas my true love gave to me five gold rings ..."

SPEAKER 5: The "five gold rings" are the first five books of the Bible, also called the Book of the Law.

ALL: (*Sing*) "On the sixth day of Christmas my true love gave to me six geese a-laying ..."

SPEAKER 6: The "six geese a-laying" are the six days of Creation.

ALL: (*Sing*) "On the seventh day of Christmas my true love gave to me seven swans a-swimming ..."

SPEAKER 7: The "seven swans a-swimming" are the seven gifts of the Holy Spirit described in Romans 12:6-8.

ALL: (*Sing*) "On the eighth day of Christmas my true love gave to me eight maids a-milking ..."

SPEAKER 8: The "eight maids a-milking" are the eight Beatitudes.

ALL: (*Sing*) "On the ninth day of Christmas my true love gave to me nine ladies dancing ..."

SPEAKER 9: The nine ladies dancing are the nine fruits of the Holy Spirit that Paul lists in Galatians 5:22-23.

ALL: (*Sing*) "On the tenth day of Christmas my true love gave to me ten lords a-leaping ..."

SPEAKER 10: The "ten lords a-leaping" symbolize the Ten Commandments.

ALL: (*Sing*) "On the eleventh day of Christmas my true love gave to me eleven pipers piping ..."

SPEAKER 11: The "eleven pipers piping" are the eleven faithful disciples.

ALL: (*Sing*) "On the twelfth day of Christmas my true love gave to me twelve drummers drumming ..."

SPEAKER 12: The "twelve drummers drumming" are the twelve points of the Apostles Creed.

NARRATOR: (*to congregation*) Please join us in singing "The Twelve Days of Christmas." We hope that from now on when you hear this song you will remember how it had its origins in the Christian faith.

A SAVIOR IS COMING!

Production Notes

Use these monologues with older elementary children or teens. Intersperse with congregational singing for a well-rounded program that takes very little preparation time.

Elizabeth's Story

I will never forget the day I found out that I was going to have a baby. My husband Zechariah and I were getting old. We had almost given up hope of having children. But God blessed us and sent us a son—a special son. Our son would be the one to prepare the way for the Messiah that God had promised to send. Our people, the Hebrew people, had been waiting for so long.

And then one day, before my baby—whom we named John—was born, my relative Mary from Nazareth came to see me. I was surprised to see her, but I soon knew that God had sent her. She had wonderful news!

Even before Mary told me, somehow I knew that she was going to be the mother of the Messiah. My baby knew it too, although I still don't understand how. "Blessed are you among women," I told her.

I know Mary must have been scared. After all, she and Joseph were not married yet. She must have worried about what people would think. And she was so young! Having a baby would be news enough, but to be the mother of God's Son was a real blessing and an awesome responsibility. But Mary's faith was strong. I could see why God had chosen her to be the mother of the Messiah. Even in her uncertainty about the future, Mary sang praises to God for blessing her.

Hymn suggestion: "My Soul Gives Glory to My God"

The Innkeeper

Hymn suggestion: "Once in Royal David's City"

I had no idea what was about to happen the night Joseph from Nazareth knocked on the door of my inn looking for a place to stay. I was sorry that Mary would not have a nice room to sleep in that night. I knew that they were tired from the long trip, but there was nothing I could do. Everyone was coming home to Bethlehem because they had to be counted in the census and pay their taxes. My inn was full. There was no room!

But thank goodness I thought of the stable. The stable was built inside a cave. Animals stayed there, but Joseph and Mary would be inside out of the night air, and the straw would make a soft bed. It was the best I could do!

I had no idea that Mary's baby would be born during the night. But she and Joseph did fine in the stable. They made a bed of straw in the manger. I would never have thought of that. The manger is the trough the animals eat their food out of. I bet they were surprised to find a newborn baby lying there.

Hymn suggestion: "The Friendly Beasts"

I didn't know right away who this newborn baby was. Joseph told me that they named him Jesus, but it was many years before I realized that Jesus was the Savior that God had promised. Now that I know that Jesus is the Messiah, I am even more glad that I didn't turn Mary and Joseph away into the night. I didn't have a room in my inn, but I am very glad that I remembered the stable and let them spend the night there. The manger made a good bed for a newborn baby.

Hymn suggestion: "He Is Born"

The Shepherd

Hymn suggestion: "Infant Holy, Infant Lowly"

I'm a shepherd near Bethlehem. Let me tell you something special that happened late one night. We had counted all the sheep and they were settled in the sheepfold and were ready for a good night's rest. The other shepherds had fallen asleep near the campfire. But I had the first watch, so I had to stay awake for awhile.

Struggling to stay awake, I thought about all the people we had seen going toward Bethlehem that day. They were going to pay their taxes just as the emperor had ordered. I remember thinking, *Bethlehem is not big enough! I hope these people can find somewhere comfortable to sleep tonight.*

I shouldn't have fallen asleep, but I guess I did. Suddenly I was awakened by a sound. I jumped up, afraid that I was about to find a wolf ready to attack my sheep. But there were no wild animals anywhere. *But what was that sound?* I wondered. Then there it was again. And this time there was a great light over everything—right in the darkest part of the night. I called to the other shepherds, "Get up! Get up!"

The others woke up startled. When they saw the light, they looked up into the sky. "What is it?" they wanted to know. We were all terrified!

But then we heard an angel's voice. "Do not be afraid," the angel said. "We have come to tell you good news of great joy for all people. Tonight the Messiah, the Savior of the world, has been born in Bethlehem!"

When the angels had gone, we started toward Bethlehem. When we found the baby, we told everyone what the angels had said: "This child born in a stable in Bethlehem is the Messiah that the Hebrew people have been waiting for these many years. Praise God! The Savior has come!"

Hymn suggestion: "O Little Town of Bethlehem"

ADVENT READINGS AND PRAYERS

First Sunday

Today is the first Sunday of Advent. Today begins a new church year. *Advent* means "arrival" or "a new beginning." The season of Advent includes the four Sundays before Christmas Day. It is a time to prepare our hearts and minds for the arrival of Jesus. It is a time of waiting for the birth of Christ. Each Sunday we will light a candle in the Advent wreath.

Read Isaiah 60:1.

Light the first candle and say: We light this candle to remember that Jesus brings us hope.

Pray: Dear God, we know that Jesus came to bring us salvation and has promised to come again. We pray that we will always be ready to welcome him. Amen.

Second Sunday

Light the first candle and say: We lighted the first candle to remember that Jesus brings us hope.

Read Mark 1:2*b*.

Light the second candle and say: We light the second candle to remember that Jesus shows us the way.

Pray: Make us willing, O God, to play our part in your great plan.Thank you for sending messengers to show us your way. Amen.

Third Sunday

Light the first candle and say: We lighted the first candle to remember that Jesus brings us hope. *Light the second candle and say:* We lighted the second candle to remember that Jesus shows us the right way.

Read Psalm 84:12.

Light the third candle and say: We light this candle to remember that Jesus brings us joy.

Pray: Dear God, we are looking forward with joy to the birth of your Son.

Fourth Sunday

Light the first candle and say: We lighted the first candle to remind us that Jesus gives us hope. *Light the second candle and say:* We lighted the second candle to remember that Jesus shows us the right way. *Light the third candle and say:* We lighted the third candle to remind us that Jesus brings us joy.

Read Isaiah 9:6.

Light the fourth candle and say: We light this candle to remind us that Jesus brings us peace.

Pray: Dear God, thank you for sending Jesus to bring peace to our world. Amen.

Amen

A - men, a - men, a - men, a - men, a - men. A -

1. See the lit - tle ba - by
2. See him in the tem - ple
3. Je - sus is my Sav - ior,

ly - ing in a man - ger one Christ - mas morn - ing.
talk - ing to the eld - ers. How they mar - veled at his wis - dom.
Je - sus died to save us, And he rose on Eas - ter.

men, a - men,

(last time)

a - men, a - men, a - men.

All voices may repeat the first "Amens" after stanza 3.

WORDS and MUSIC: African American spiritual; harm. by J. Jefferson Cleveland and Verolga Nix; adapt. by Nylea L. Butler-Moore.
Harm. © 1981 Abingdon Press; adapt. © 1993 Abingdon Press

An Angel Told Mary

1. An an - gel told Ma - ry good news, good news!
2. ___ She would name him Je - sus, good news, good news!

She would have a ba - by, good news, good news!
He would show God's love, ___ good news, good news!

WORDS and MUSIC: Diane C. G. Garrison
© 1990 Graded Press

Glory!

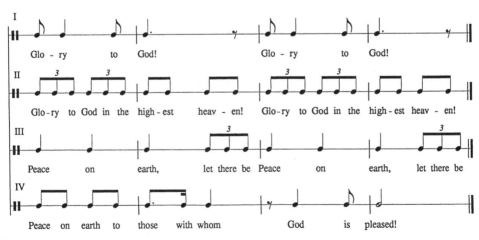

I Glo - ry to God! Glo - ry to God!

II Glo - ry to God in the high - est heav - en! Glo - ry to God in the high - est heav - en!

III Peace on earth, let there be Peace on earth, let there be

IV Peace on earth to those with whom God is pleased!

WORDS: Luke 2:14 (adapted)
MUSIC: James Ritchie
Music copyright © 1990 by Graded Press

Holy Baby, Holy Child

WORDS and MUSIC: Lynn S. Hurst